*Isha Upanishad
and Commentary*

By
Charles Johnston

Copyright © 2020 Lamp of Trismegistus. All rights reserved. No part of this publication may be reproduced or transmitted in any form or by any means, electronic or mechanical, including photocopying, recording, or by any information storage and retrieval system, without permission in writing from Lamp of Trismegistus. Reviewers may quote brief passages.

ISBN: 978-1-63118-490-1

*Esoteric Classics:
Eastern Studies*

Other Books in this Series and Related Titles

Kena Upanishad and Commentary by Charles Johnston (978-1-63118-491-8)

Katha Upanishad and Commentary by Charles Johnston (978-1-63118-493-2)

Prashna Upanishad and Commentary by Charles Johnston (978-1-63118-494-9)

Atma Bodha & Tattva Bodha by Adi Shankara &c (978-1-63118-401-7)

The Crest-Jewel of Wisdom by Adi Shankara (978-1-63118-475-8)

Catholicism, Yoga and Hinduism by Hartmann &c (978-1-63118-478-9)

Yoga, Hatha-Yoga and Raja-Yoga by Annie Besant (978-1-63118-476-5)

The Tree of Wisdom by Nagarjuna (978-1-63118-470-3)

The Path of Light: A Manual of Maha-Yana Buddhism (978-1-63118-471-0)

Buddhist Psalms by Shinran (978-1-63118-465-9)

Tao Te Ching & Commentary by Lao Tzu & C Johnston (978-1-63118-495-6)

The Hymns of Hermes by G. R. S. Mead (978-1-63118-405-5)

The Golden Verses of Pythagoras: Five Translations (978-1-63118-479-6)

Gnosis of the Mind by G. R. S. Mead (978-1-63118-408-6)

The Hymn of Jesus by G. R. S. Mead (978-1-63118-492-5)

The Book of the Watchers by Enoch (978-1-63118-416-1)

The Secrets of Enoch by Enoch (978-1-63118-449-9)

The Gospel of the Nativity of Mary by St. Matthew (978-1-63118-448-2)

Clairvoyance and Psychic Abilities by A Besant &c (978-1-63118-403-1)

A Collection of Early Writings on Astral Travel (978-1-63118-477-2)

The Sepher Yetzirah and the Qabalah by M P Hall (978-1-63118-481-9)

Audio versions are also available on Audible, Amazon and Apple

Table of Contents

Introduction...7

Isha Upanishad
Translated by Charles Johnston...9

"By the Master"
Commentary on the Isha Upanishad
By Charles Johnston...13

Ishopanishad
Translated by Raja Ram Mohun Roy...47

INTRODUCTION

The word "esoteric" can be difficult to define. Esotericism in general can be seen less as a system of beliefs and more as a category, which encompasses numerous, different systems of beliefs. It's a bit of juxtaposition, since the word "esoteric" indicates something that few people know about, while the term itself broadly covers numerous philosophies, practices, areas of study and belief systems.

In a greater sense, Esotericism acts as a storehouse for secret knowledge, which is often considered ancient *(by tradition, if not by fact),* passed down from generation to generation, in private. At various times in history, simply possessing the knowledge of some of these subjects, was considered illegal and a jailable offence, if discovered. This usually included such general topics as Alchemy, Pharmacology, Qabalah, Hermeticism, Occultism, Ceremonial Magic, Astrology, Divination, Rosicrucianism and so on. Collectively, these areas of study were often referred to as the esoteric sciences.

Sometimes, the outer garment of a subject isn't esoteric, while what is hidden beneath it, is. As an example, Freemasonry isn't necessarily esoteric by nature (at *least not anymore),* but certain signs, passwords and handshakes given to the candidate during their initiation, are in fact, esoteric, in the sense that they are hidden from the general public.

Today, in the twenty-first century, such topics are readily available at bookstores across the country, and numerous mainsteam publishers offer beginners guides and coffee-table volumes on many of these subjects, intended for mass appeal. Books like *"The Secret"* have turned previously arcane topics into household knowledge. All that being the case, however, it isn't to say that there still aren't buried secrets to uncover, ancient wisdom being ignored and forgotten mysteries to be explored. In fact, it is often that we are only able to further our own studies by standing on the shoulders of these disappearing giants.

Lamp of Trismegistus is doing its part to help preserve humanity's esoteric history by making some of these classics available to those students who are seeking to unearth the knowledge of these ancient colossi.

So, be sure to check other titles from our *Esoteric Classics* series, as well as our *Occult Fiction*, *Theosophical Classics*, *Foundations of Freemasonry Series*, *Supernatural Fiction*, *Paranormal Research Series*, *Studies in Buddhism* and our *Christian Apocrypha Series*. You can also download the audio versions of most of these titles from Amazon, Apple or Audible, for learning on the go.

ISHA UPANISHAD

Translated by Charles Johnston

By the Master all this is to be clothed and pervaded, whatever moves in this moving world.

Through this renounced, thou shalt enjoy; covet not the wealth of any!

Toiling, therefore, here at his tasks, let him be willing to live a hundred ages; this is it with thee, and not otherwise, nor does work smear and befoul the man.

Sunless, verily, are those worlds, by blind darkness enwrapped; they enter into those worlds on going forth—the men who are slayers of their own souls.

Without moving, that One is swifter than mind. Nor did the bright Powers overtake It; It went swiftly before them. That outstrips the others, though they run, while It stands still. In That Matarishvan disposes the life-streams.

That moves, That moves not; That is afar off, That is as if near. That is within all this; That is outside all this.

But he who beholds all beings in the supreme Self (Atma), and in all beings beholds the supreme Self, does not seek to hide himself from That.

In whom all beings have become as the Self of the enlightened, what delusion is there, what sorrow, for him beholding Oneness?

He circled around the bright, bodiless, woundless, without tendons, pure, unpierced by evil; the wise Poet, all-encircling, self-being, disposing ends through perpetual ages.

They go forth into blind darkness, who worship unwisdom; but into darkness deeper than that, as it were, they who find delight in wisdom.

There is one thing, they have said, through wisdom; there is another thing, they have said, through unwisdom. Thus have we heard from the wise, who have taught us the spiritual teaching.

He who knows both, wisdom and unwisdom, he, verily, through unwisdom fording through death, through wisdom reaches the Immortal.

They go forth into blind darkness, who worship that which is not the Life; but into darkness deeper than that, as it were, they who find delight in the Life.

There is one thing, they have said, through the Life; there is another thing, they have said, through that which is not the Life.

Thus have we heard from the wise, who taught us the spiritual teachings.

He who knows both, the Life and destruction, through destruction fording through death, through the Life reaches the Immortal.

By a veil as of gold, the face of the Real is hidden. O thou Shepherd of the flock, Lord of the sun, lift up that veil, for the vision of the law of the Real!

Shepherd and Lord of Light, thou Only Seer, Lord of Death, Light-Giver, Son of the Lord of Life, send forth thy rays and bring them together!

That radiance of thine, thy form most beautiful I behold; the Spiritual Man in the real world. That am I!

My Spirit enters the Spirit, the Immortal. And this body has its end in ashes.

O Sacrifice, remember! Remember what has been done! O Sacrifice, remember! Remember what has been done!

O Divine Fire, lead us by the good path to Victory! O Bright One, thou who knowest all wisdoms!

Give us victory over our consuming sin! To Thee we offer the highest word of praise!

"BY THE MASTER"

ISHA Upanishad

Translated from the Sanskrit with an Interpretation

By the Master all this is to be clothed and pervaded, whatever moves in this moving world.

These words, like all that is of primary value in the great Upanishads, are addressed to the disciple. For the consciousness of the disciple, the Master here is the Warrior, the consciousness and will of the inner Self. But this consciousness and will is in reality one with the will and consciousness of the Master of that disciple; the will and consciousness of the Logos, as expressed and embodied in that Master.

It is not that the disciple must follow out all his own thoughts and volitions, attributing these to his Master; it is rather that he must, through sacrifice and purification, discern within himself those thoughts and volitions, those intuitions of perception and action which really come from his Master, and seek courageously and with devotion to carry these out, in every task and situation which comes before him. In this way, through aspiration, sacrifice, and devotion, and through ceaselessly valorous action, his own individual nature, the inner and the outer, is to be clothed and infused by the Master.

But the teaching has a still wider scope. He must perceive the Master in everyone with whom he comes in contact. The man or woman or child to whom he is speaking, with whom he is acting, must be for him the Master; he must speak and act towards that person as to the Master.

Does this mean that the disciple must take every word and act of everyone with whom he comes in contact as being the words and acts of his Master? In one sense, yes; but only when the matter is rightly and profoundly understood. The principle of discernment has already been indicated: just as, when dealing with his own nature, he must not take all thoughts and volitions which arise in it as being the thoughts and volitions of his Master; but must, on the contrary, with sacrifice and devotion seek out and discern the Master's thought and will for him; so, in dealing with another he must, with equal sacrifice and courage, with the entire disinterestedness of detachment, seek and discern the Master's thought and will for that person. To put it in another way: he must seek and discern the Master's ideal for that person and work courageously to carry that ideal toward realization. Since the Master has an ideal for each man, woman, or child with whom his disciple comes in contact, both a general ideal reaching toward ultimate perfection and divinity, and a particular ideal for that time and situation, therefore the Master, as that ideal, is in that person, and the disciple must behold him there, and must act, at once with valour and with humility, on that vision of his Master. Therefore by the Master is to be clothed and pervaded, first the inner and outer nature of the disciple himself; next, the man, woman, or child with whom he is in contact, whether in speech or action.

This appears to be the meaning of the religious injunction, that the disciple must see God in the person with whom he is speaking, towards whom he is acting, whether that person be a superior, an equal or an inferior, a saint or a sinner. There are no exceptions whatever.

Therefore we find a Master saying: I was an hungered, and ye gave me meat: I was thirsty, and ye gave me drink: I was a stranger, and ye took me in: naked, and ye clothed me: I was sick, and ye visited me: I was in prison, and ye came unto me. Then shall the righteous answer him, saying, Lord, when saw we thee an hungered, and fed thee? or thirsty, and gave thee drink? When saw we thee a stranger, and took thee in? or naked, and clothed thee? Or when saw we thee sick, or in prison, and came unto thee? And the King shall answer and say unto them, Verily I say unto you, Inasmuch as ye have done it unto one of the least of these my brethren, ye have done it unto me.

This must be carried out, therefore, with the literalness and completeness with which the Master has here stated it. So vital and far-reaching is this principle, that the Master makes it the sole condition of salvation, of spiritual life.

Besides oneself and one's neighbour, there is a third field in which this principle and method must be applied by the disciple: whatever moves in this moving world. All this must be clothed and pervaded by the Master. He must see his Master literally in everything; in the situation, circumstances and events of his own personal life, without any exception whatever; in the situation, circumstances and events of the whole world. It is hardly necessary to say that this does not mean that his own

Master actually decides and directs all mundane and cosmic events, in any arbitrary and personal sense. But his Master's consciousness is the expression of the consciousness of the Lodge, of the Logos; his Master's will is the will of the Lodge, of the Logos. And therefore that which is the essence of his Master's will and consciousness does in fact decide and direct all mundane and cosmic events. Further, the disciple has his approach to the will and consciousness of the Lodge, of the Logos, through his own Master. His task is, to endeavour to perceive and to affect all events with the vision and will of his own Master; to become, through sacrifice and devotion, one with the consciousness and will of that Master.

In this way, then, by the Master all this is to be clothed and pervaded, whatever moves in the moving world: first, the inner nature of the disciple; then his neighbour; then all outer events without exception.

Through this renounced, thou shalt enjoy, covet not the wealth of any!

It is curious that this sentence contains the whole problem of the twentieth century, with its solution; curious, since the words were written in Sanskrit not only twenty centuries ago, but perhaps, more nearly twenty milleniums. The sentences of the Lodge are everlasting, and this is one of them.

The whole problem of the twentieth century,—since the vice of the age is covetousness. Covetousness, the angry desire to be in the situation and circumstances belonging to another, whether another man or another nation. But these circumstances, that situation, were assigned to the man, to the nation, by the will of the Lodge, the embodied Logos; assigned to him, not to us. And our situation, our circumstances, were, by the same will of the Lodge, the Logos, assigned to us, not to him; assigned, in each case, because the soul imperatively requires, for its present learning, exactly that situation, those circumstances. The law is as simple as simplicity itself.

But before we can understand this or any other spiritual law, we must first obey it with measurable completeness. We must accept our circumstances, with patience and sacrifice, before we can possibly understand them. In the footsteps of devoted acceptance will come understanding, and this understanding will steadily broaden and deepen, until we see the full purpose of the Master, and why, in wise compassion, he gave us just that situation, just these circumstances.

We must accept before we can understand; and this means the cheerful acceptance of the whole heart, not a grudging, resentful resignation. And we must begin by accepting, as the key of the situation, the centre of all circumstances, the Master himself; each one, the Master who set him in the midst of those circumstances, the reality of that Master, the excellence of his will. We must, if we would make any genuine progress, begin with the Master. Therefore this Upanishad begins with the Master.

There are two false beginnings. To begin with self, means to end in death. To begin with our neighbour, means to end in confusion. We must, if we would begin wisely, begin with the Master, accepting his compassionate will, seeking his purposes that we may fulfil them. To prefer the will of the Master to one's own will in any one thing, is the beginning of discipleship. He who prefers the Master's will to his own will, not only in one thing, but in all, is already an accepted disciple.

Through this renunciation, the disciple will find joy; by preferring, at each point, the Master's will to his own will. Joy, for this reason: the Master's will for him is the will of the Logos, the will of infinite wisdom, infinite compassion, infinite Love. To conform to the purpose of that wisdom, that love, is the very essence of joy. Who could live, who could breathe, asks another Upanishad, if the heart of Being were not joy?

Exactly the same law is enunciated again and again, by the western Master already quoted: He that loveth his life shall lose it: he that hateth his life shall keep it unto life eternal. To love the personal life, the life of the lower will and inclinations, self-centred and greedy, is to stake everything on that which is already condemned to death. To hate that lower life in us, because of its greed, its baseness, its ruthless readiness to sacrifice others, its vanity and consequent treachery; and, hating that, to love with passionate ardour the will of the Master in us and for us, because of its holiness, its purity, its loveliness, its compassion for us and others, and, even more, because the Master's will is the very essence of self-sacrifice, an age-long offering, in virtue of which alone he is a Master; to love that life with the heart's whole ardour, is already to have a place in eternal life.

Toiling, therefore, here at his tasks, let him be willing to live a hundred ages; this is it with thee, and not otherwise, nor does work smear and befoul the man.

A word may be said here concerning the real nature of this Upanishad. It is, if you wish, a philosophical treatise; further, it is a Mystery teaching. But it appears to be even more: a ritual or rather fragments of a ritual of one of the great Initiations.

Certain tasks for the disciple have already been outlined in the preceding sentences of the Upanishad. And it has been said that before the disciple can at all understand the inner meaning of any one of these tasks, the Master's purpose for him in that task, he must have carried it through with measurable completeness. So there are, for the disciple of a given stature, in each stage of his journey homeward, a group of tasks, the entire course of spiritual studies and undertakings for that stage or class. Each of these must be carried through with entire faithfulness, with measurable completeness, before the inner significance of the course, and its relation to the whole of divine life, can be understood and seen in the light of illumined spiritual vision.

When the course for that stage and stature is completed, the Lodge takes it upon itself to bring to the disciple the full revelation of its significance, its meaning and purpose in the light of eternity. And this is done in what is at once a Lodge ceremony and a tremendous spiritual experience, wherein the disciple, while taking a part in certain forms and symbolic acts and words, at the same time is rapt into the full consciousness of his own Master, of that Master's Master, and of the whole splendid chain of Immortals, up to, and including, the full divine consciousness of Nirvana. Such a ritual, or a part of such a ritual, this Upanishad would appear to be. It was put in form, no doubt, millenniums ago, before the red Rajput race, who were the possessors of the Mysteries in older India, left their earlier home in Egypt; perhaps before the race which formed the illumined nucleus of Egypt came thither from still unfallen Atlantis. For, as the realities of the Lodge are from everlasting to everlasting, so are its Mysteries and symbols, its supremely spiritual symbolic ceremonies.

If one keeps in mind what thus appears to be the real character of this Upanishad, one will be better able to understand the full meaning of the verse just translated. From the very inception, the life of the disciple is sacrifice; each step of the long journey is sacrifice; its consummation, the end of the way, is supreme sacrifice. The whole history of that life is told, with the simplicity which comes only from complete mastery, by a Master, in *Light on the Path*; and it is made clear that the first part of the way involves the sacrifice of renunciation, the putting off of the old man, as Paul the Initiate phrases it. The next stage of the way involves the sacrifice of valour, heroic toil, the putting on of the new man; the painful and difficult evocation of the dormant divine powers and faculties, and their application to their tasks; something that can be done only by dauntless, indefatigable will, with boundless courage and faith in one's Master; something that cannot even be attempted, until the first part of the way, the putting off of the old man, has been measurably carried through.

It is easy to see why this is. If the divine forces were evoked, aroused, and brought into activity, while the impulses and substance of the old man remained, this would mean the inflaming and intoxication of that lingering lower nature by these potent forces. The outcome would be the creation of a powerful devil; not salvation, but swift damnation. Therefore such a great part of all published scriptures is concerned with the first part of the way, the stage of painful self-conquest, of purification, during which the whole personality must be dissolved. Only after this has been done, can the disciple gain any glimpse of the next stage of the way. Only after it has been done can the disciple with complete safety learn that there is a further stage of the way.

It should be clearly understood that, while this second stage is one of upbuilding, of the evoking and using of divine forces, it is none the less a way of sacrifice. For an example, to call forth courage from timidity is a peculiarly painful sacrifice, one that is bitterly trying at the beginning. In like manner, to bring heroic zeal in the place of sloth is painful, and always a sacrifice, whether bodily or intellectual sloth be the point of attack. In general, it may be said that the temper needed for this, the second stage of the way, is that of the soldier "going over the top". A part of his nature, a deep-seated tendency or weakness, will be slain in the charge.

But there is a larger sense in which the more advanced stages of the way are marked by ceaseless sacrifice. The advanced disciple and, far more, the Master, must make war on weakness and sin in the world, in others. This cannot be done from without. It must be done from within. The Master must be fully conscious of the sin, the temptations, of those whom he seeks to help; he must share the consciousness, the feeling, that urges and entices them toward that sin; and thus feeling it, he must combat it by the contrary power in his own nature. It would seem to be this law, this process, that the Buddha had in mind, when he said: "Let the sins of Kali Yuga rest on me, but let man be saved!" In this sense, therefore, must the disciple be willing to toil through "a hundred ages", taking up, as his Master took up so long ago, that terrible toil which is, nevertheless, a great and ever-increasing delight.

And as the Master, while fully conscious of the feeling of allurement which the sin he is combating has for the sinner, is, by virtue of his inherent purity, free from the least enticement, so must the disciple understand that the great and terrible toil for others cannot lead to impurity, if his own heart be pure.

There is a final and supreme point at which the sacrifice of freely accepted toil, of immersion, almost, in the sins and temptations of the world, must be assumed: when, at the last initiation, the Master puts aside the well-earned peace and silence of Nirvana, and undertakes instead to lift and bear a part of the "heavy Karma of the world". Of every Master at this point it will be true that "he is tempted at all points, yet without sin". The incarnation of an Avatar is the type and symbol, as well as the actuality of this sacrifice, but it is equally real for all other Masters, who remain unseen, in what, for the rest of mankind, is the impenetrable darkness of the occult world.

The Upanishad text continues:

Sunless, verily, are those worlds, by blind darkness enwrapped; they enter into those worlds on going forth— the men who are slayers of their own souls.

As through ceaseless sacrifice the disciple is bringing his soul to life, enkindling within himself the long dormant divine elements, so there are those who, by continued refusal of sacrifice, in fact sacrifice the higher to the lower self, and thereby literally slay their souls. It would appear that every initiation must contain, in its ritual, some such warning of the penalty of failure and betrayal; for the real failure comes only through deliberate sin.

So the disciple, in this initiation which in fact sums up the long path of toil and sacrifice which he has travelled, and at the same time lights up with divine radiance the splendid way before him, is made to see what would have been the penalty of failure, if through baseness he had made the great betrayal. He would have fallen into those worlds, by blind darkness enwrapped, which await those who sin against the light, who are guilty of the sin against the Holy Ghost, the divine element within themselves. Speaking of this divine element, the Upanishad continues:

Without moving, that One is swifter than mind. Nor did the bright Powers overtake It; It went swiftly before them. That outstrips the others, though they run, while It stands still. In That Matarishvan disposes the life-streams.

At this stage of the initiation, the disciple is being initiated into the consciousness of the divine element within himself, the principle which is called Buddhi, and which may be thought of as the active potency and manifestation of Atma.

It has already become clear that the same law holds good for the initiation of the disciple and the initiation of the Master, once allowance is made for difference of degree. There is one point at which the analogy is completely true, though it may not be always realized: just as there are difficulties and perplexing problems for the disciple, which can only be solved by courage and endurance and humility, and even then solved practically, rather than comprehended, so, on their own evidence, there are difficulties and even insolvable problems for the Masters themselves, which they approach by the same path of courage and humility, finding a working method, rather than a full comprehension. And no matter what lofty peak of spiritual splendour may be reached, the depths of the sky will still be as far above it; there will ever be deeper and greater mysteries.

This is in the nature of things. Sir Oliver Lodge has been quoted as saying that Science asks questions which will never be answered. And it must be so, even when it is a question of the greatest Masters. For it is in the nature of things impossible that Being should go behind Being, to discover why Being is. It is in the nature of things impossible that Consciousness should observe the causes which bring Consciousness into being, or detect the source from which Consciousness springs. That is insolvable and will remain insolvable for ever.

That divine and mysterious principle which lies behind manifested consciousness, and from which consciousness springs, is, in its unmanifested form, ever unknowable. It is in essence one with Parabrahm, the eternally Unknowable. Therefore it is said that this mysterious One is swifter than mind, swifter than thought. However swiftly thought may move, the mysteriousness of the One is there before it; the mystery still remains a mystery. It perpetually outstrips the mind's bright powers. However far the plummet may descend, there are still the unfathomable depths beyond.

But while unknowable in its unmanifested form, the divine element is knowable in its manifested form; Atma is knowable when it is revealed as Buddhi. And in a certain sense it is true that the whole process of initiation is simply the progressive revelation of Buddhi in the consciousness of the disciple. This may help us to realize what a tremendous and vital thing the principle we call Buddhi is.

We know Buddhi, so far, through its two reflections: Prana and Kama. If we consider Prana alone, how immense is its scope, as the sustaining power of all vegetable and animal life throughout the world, the "vital fire," in its simplest form; yet, though in its simplest form, ceaselessly working miracles.

But what we have now to realize, what the disciple has to realize at the point we are considering is, that all the miracles of the manifested world, wrought out by Prana, the Life-force, are no more than reflections of the real miracles of Buddhi, into which he is now to be initiated by progressive degrees.

It would be well to understand at the outset, that, just as with the seven principles, the lower six are synthesized by the seventh, Atma; so with each principle: it has six aspects, powers, sub-principles, whatever we may agree to call them, which are synthesized by the seventh; these sub-principles exactly corresponding, under the universal law of Correspondence, to the primary principles.

Thus the principle with which we are now concerned, the "divine fire", Buddhi, should be regarded as containing, or consisting of, seven sub-principles, six of which are synthesized by the seventh; this group of seven sub-principles accurately corresponding to the seven primary principles.

The sub-principles of Buddhi have been described as the seven Shaktis, or spiritual powers. For our present purpose, we need only consider the four higher Shaktis : Ichchha shakti, which is the sub-principle of Buddhi corresponding to Kama; Kriya shakti, the sub-principle of Buddhi corresponding to Manas; Kundalini shakti, the sub-principle of Buddhi corresponding to Buddhi itself; and Mantrika shakti, the sub-principle of Buddhi corresponding to Atma, and synthesizing the six.

In a certain sense, the task before the disciple is the evocation of the "divine fire", Kundalini, and the infusion of the principle of Will in him by that divine fire; the golden light mingling with the red flame, to produce the colour of the mystic rose. The fiery aspiration of the disciple evokes the higher celestial fire, and the two blend in one, the holy fire which shall thereafter illumine and enkindle that disciple's heart and life and every act.

This awakened divine fire is intuition, creative genius, the essence of aspiration; it infuses itself into Kriya shakti (the sub-principle of Buddhi which corresponds to Manas), the power of imagination and thought. Imagination then becomes the power to give form to divine intuition and inspiration, whether that form be in words or any other vehicle of representation; and thought, inspired by the divine light, becomes prophetic, formulating the plans and purposes of the Eternal.

This evocation of Buddhi, this arousing of the divine fire by sacrifice and aspiration, is the mystical meaning within the story of Prometheus, who brought down divine fire to men; and Prometheus has his prototype in Matarishvan, the Vedic Prometheus, who brought down the divine fire for the Bhrigus, as told in the sixtieth hymn of the first circle of the Rig Veda.

That moves, That moves not; That is afar off, That is as if near. That is within all this; That is outside all this.

Here, as always when it is a question of the Logos, a description can be given only in terms of paradox. One finds exactly the same thing in the Tao-Teh-King, on page after page, when Lao-Tse seeks to indicate the Way, which is his name for the nameless Mind of God. Thus, for example, one finds Lao-Tse saying: "Therefore those of old said: who has the light of the Way, seems wrapped in darkness; who has advanced along the Way, seems backward; who has mounted the Way, seems of low estate."

Perhaps the best solution of this problem of paradox can be given along the lines of that deeply intuitive half-Oriental, Bergson, who so constantly, and as unconsciously, approaches the thought and even the words of the great Upanishads. The

Ultimate Reality, which Bergson, in this also following the Upanishads, calls the Life, approaches our consciousness in two ways, from two directions: inwardly, through the spiritual consciousness which Bergson calls the intuition; and outwardly, from the visible universe, through the material mind. The analysis of the material mind is, perhaps, Bergson's most valuable achievement. It is, he says, an instrument of consciousness, gradually built up in contact with the forms and forces of the material world, and exactly fitted, by its character and habit, to deal practically with the problems and situations of the material world, the world expressing itself in terms of time and space. But, just because the material mind is so perfectly adapted to this practical, material task, it is by the very reason of this perfect adaptation, quite unable to tackle successfully the problems of direct spiritual consciousness, of Reality. The dominant thought of Bergson is that, although the material mind is by its very nature unfitted to grapple with the problem of Reality, we are not for that reason cut off from the knowledge of Reality; on the contrary, the consciousness of the Real, the spiritual consciousness, which Bergson calls intuition, is the very heart and centre of our nature; the consciousness of Life, which is the consciousness of the Logos, is present within us perpetually.

We can easily work out in detail the contrast between these two forms of consciousness: intuition and the material mind, as Bergson himself does. Intuition perceives the universe as Life, the great forward movement of Being. The material mind sees the universe as a congeries of material forms, each material form having the air of permanence. Bergson has found an apt simile for this contrast, in the films of moving pictures: the material mind sees the separate fixed pictures, as they are on the ribbon of the film; intuition, on the contrary, sees the picture on the screen, life, perpetually moving forward. Again, the intuition perceives Life as eternal duration; the material mind cuts life up into sections of time, past, present and future, which sections bear to each other exactly the relation of successive sections of the moving-picture film. Finally, intuition perceives Life as immediate, as present spiritual consciousness; while the material mind sees the universe projected in space; and, thus seeing it, is launched on an endless sea of contradictions. For example, when we think of the universe as extended in space, it is quite impossible for us, as Herbert Spencer pointed out, either to imagine a boundary at the outer edge of space, or to imagine space without a boundary. On considerations of this kind Herbert Spencer built his teaching of the Unknowable. Bergson replies in effect: Yes, unknowable, to the material mind, which was never intended to solve problems of that kind, but is simply a piece of practical machinery; unknowable to the mind, but easily knowable, and in fact already intimately known, by the intuition.

Applying Bergson's solution, we may now try to unravel the paradox of the Upanishad sentence thus:

"The Reality moves, because it is seen by the material mind projected in space; it moves not, because it is always present to the intuition, as spiritual consciousness, as Life. That is afar off, because the material mind projects Reality into space, in a universe which it is unable to conceive as either with or without boundaries. That is as if near, because it is within, as spiritual consciousness. That Logos is within all this, as the inner spiritual consciousness; it is outside all this, since the material mind conceives a universe extended in space, and containing everything that is in space."

Bergson clearly sees the antithesis between intuition and the material mind, as two modes of perception; the contrast between the "noëtic" action of intuition and the "psychic" action of the material mind. This is the strength of his philosophy. Its weakness lies in the fact that he is inclined always to see this antithesis in terms of perception, while the vital thing is, to see it in terms of action, as a moral rather than a mental problem. Either he does not see, or he does not make sufficiently clear, the fundamental truth that not merely the perceptive faculty of the material mind, but the whole lower, personal nature has been built up in contact with matter and the things of matter; that the whole personal nature is, therefore, false to reality; that the passions and desires and, above all, the dominating impulse of egotism, are the expression of this false building; and that this false building must come down, before the real dwelling-place of the soul can be built.

This unbuilding of the false lower nature, in order that the true higher nature may be built up, is the fundamental task of our moral and religious life. It is the central work of the Mysteries; and the series of Initiations exists solely to carry this work into practical effect. It is, therefore, the theme which runs through all the great Upanishads, which are the records of the Mysteries, and of Initiation.

As a contrast to the purely mental antithesis between the intuition and the material mind which is so lucidly indicated by Bergson, we may quote an equally lucid statement of the same antithesis, this time in moral rather than mental terms; in terms of the will, rather than in terms of action:

"For we know that the law is spiritual: but I am carnal, sold under sin. For that which I work I know not: for not what I would, that do I practise; but what I hate, that I do. But if what I would not, that I do, I consent unto the law that it is good. So now it is no more I that work it, but sin which dwelleth in me. For I know that in me, that is, in my flesh, dwelleth no good thing: for to will is present with me, but to work that which is good is not. For the good which I would I do not: but the evil which I would not, that I practise. But if what I would not, that I do, it is no more I that work it, but sin which dwelleth in me. I find then the law, that, to me who would do good, evil is present. For I delight in the law of God after the inward man: but I see a different law in my members, warring against the law of my mind, and bringing me into captivity under the law of sin which is in my members. O wretched man that I am! Who shall deliver me out of this body of death?" (Romans, 7, 14-24, Revised version with marginal readings.)

That is really the statement of our whole practical problem. The solution is, humbly and faithfully and through sacrifice, to co-operate with the powers of the manifested Logos, with the Masters, who are perpetually striving to work for us just this deliverance.

Mental understanding will amount to nothing, until it is consecrated by sacrifice. More than that, even a true mental insight, if not so consecrated, will presently be veiled and lost, the power of Maya once more asserting itself. Therefore the word "sin" comes closer to the heart of the matter than does Bergson's analysis of the material mind. The realization of sin is far more vital than the realization of mental illusion; and indeed the realization of mental illusion is only valuable because it may help to break down the self-sufficiency of the material mind, with its perpetual tendency to self-justification. But the real task is for the will, and it can be accomplished only through painful sacrifice.

But he who beholds all beings in the supreme Self (Atma), and in all beings beholds the supreme Self, does not seek to hide himself from That.

The kernel and centre of the lower nature, the "body of death," is egotism, the self-centered consciousness which practically believes itself to be the centre of the universe, that for whose sake all things exist. Thus believing, thus practically worshipping self-satisfaction, the egotism will, in practice, sacrifice all other beings to itself; and will, so far as it is able, sacrifice the spiritual consciousness, which is in fact the power of the Logos, to the carnal consciousness.

There would seem to be two ways in which the egotism can be conquered: an apparent and temporary way, and a real and permanent way. The unreal and unenduring way is, without regard to the Logos, without regard to the law of God and holiness, to attempt to sacrifice the egotism to other people. As

Lao-Tse dryly puts it: "When the Way (the immediate spiritual consciousness of the Logos, the Master) is lost, the form of virtue takes it place. When the lower virtue is lost, humanitarianism takes it place." The practical working-out of this unspiritual humanitarianism is seen in Socialism, in the abominations of Bolshevism, which has been rightly described as "Socialism in action." The reason is, that there has been no true sacrifice of egotism; the devil, only apparently cast out, returns, and brings "seven other spirits more wicked than himself, and they enter in and dwell there: and the last state of that man is worse than the first."

The only lasting conquest is to sacrifice egotism to the divine consciousness of the Logos, to sacrifice self to the Master; and, thereafter, through the power and inspiration of the Logos, revealed in the penitent heart, to follow out in all things, not the will of self, but the will of the Logos.

In this way, the disciple finds the Logos, the supreme Self, Atma, within himself; and, finding the Logos there, and step by step coming to share in the consciousness and life of the Logos, he comes into some understanding of the depth and breadth of that great spiritual Life. He comes to realize that the Logos is in all things; that it is through the virtue of that presence, that all things exist and have their being; so that "all things were made through the Logos and without the Logos was not anything made that was made." Thus he "beholds all beings in the Logos, in Atma, and in all beings beholds the Logos." The practical application, the way in which the disciple should see the Master in all beings, has already been discussed in the commentary on an earlier verse.

With reference to the last words of the verse, it would be well to consider how far we do "seek to hide ourselves from" the Logos, the divine spirit, the Master. If we realize, even mentally, that the life of the Logos is not only the real Self of us, our most real Self, but is, in essence, full of divine beauty and goodness and truth, full of everlasting love and joy; then is it not true that we are in fact, if we cling to our personal selves, seeking to hide from divine beauty, from divine goodness, from divine truth and love and joy?

We need more faith; we need the faith to surrender ourselves, and to surrender with completeness.

In whom all beings have become as the Self of the enlightened, what delusion is there, what sorrow, for him beholding Oneness?

Fear lies at the very heart of egotism: the self's fear that it will be deprived of its desires, of its illusions of vanity and superiority, even of its very being. Fear and desire go hand in hand, and each desire has an equal shadow of fear. Self-centred egotism is small, and feels itself to be small, with an ever more restricted circle of life: and, shut up in this narrow cave, egotism is constantly on guard against apprehended attacks, for nothing is so vulnerable as vanity, which is the very breath of egotism. All this means misery, dread of loss, of suffering, of punishment, a haunting misgiving and apprehension.

But when egotism is sacrificed to the Logos; when, instead of the bitter waters of selfishness, the soul is refreshed with the waters of life, springing up in a living fountain in the heart, then the age-old spectre of fear is exorcised; dread ceases to haunt the dwelling, unless it be the wise and holy fear of falling short of the high perfection, the holy Life, which offers itself so generously to the cleansed heart. But that fear is in reality worship, and has nothing in common with the old egotistic dread.

In that holy Life, all the sorrows that dwell in the heart have their surcease, except the divine sorrow which is of the very essence of that great Life: the perpetual travail, the pain of bringing holiness into being, in obdurate human hearts; the burden of the age-old task, taken up when the Logos first entered into manifestation; the task more visibly assumed, when the Logos "becomes flesh and dwells among us."

He circled around the bright, bodiless, woundless, without tendons, pure, unpierced by evil; the wise Poet, all-encircling, self-being, disposing ends through perpetual ages.

Here, it would seem, is a part of the ritual depicting the Logos as the active Builder of the worlds, "running circular errands" through the celestial ether, which is "bodiless, woundless, without tendons, pure, unpierced by evil."

Western astronomy, while measuring with wonderful insight and patience, the circling motions of the planets in their orbits about the sun, and extending these measurements not only to the distances of the stars, but to their proper motion in space, has never even attempted to find any cause or source of these vast and endless movements. Laplace, perfecting his nebular hypothesis, thought of the solar system as at first a vast sphere of star-dust, rotating about an axis; gradual flattening and shrinking, forming rings, like the rings of Saturn, which in time, breaking up, became the planets. Laplace thought that, if the original impulse of rotation could be explained, he could then account for all the phenomena of the solar system. But no explanation of that original rotation was ever forthcoming, except, perhaps, those which based it upon the collisions of earlier suns; but, even then, the prior motions of these remained unaccounted for.

The Eastern wisdom offers no final explanation, since, penetrating deeper into the universal mystery, it finds only mystery more profound. But it does carry the problem farther back, behind the visible stars and the visible universe, to the manifested Logos, which, in turn, veils the unmanifested Logos. And in the principle of circulating life within the Logos, it sees the source and cause and model of all life-circuits, from the pulsating vital current throughout the solar system, or vaster star systems, to the circulation of blood in the human body, or in the body, let us say, of a humming bird.

The Power which "circled around the bright, bodiless, woundless" ether, or rather the Akasha, is called, in the Trans-Himalyan schools, Fohat, who is described as "running circular errands," these same paths of circulation, universal from the greatest to the least, which have just been indicated. Fohat is called "the wise Poet, Seer," for, in Sanskrit, the one word covers both thoughts; he is no true poet, who is not a genuine seer; he is no true seer, who does not turn his vision into creative action. This Power of the Logos is the Poet of the star systems, of the galaxies, of the suns; and of all organized life through all these systems, where all is Life. The universe is God's poem; the voice of Life is not a cry but a song. This is the universal testimony of the Mysteries of Initiation, throughout all ages, in all lands. This wise Poet disposes all purposes and aims, and the whole substance of being, with infinite wisdom, throughout perpetual ages.

They go forth into blind darkness, who worship unwisdom; but into darkness deeper than that, as it were, they who find delight in wisdom.

The traditional interpretation found in the Indian commentaries seeks to make the point that, while they who follow unwisdom go into the darkness of death and recurring birth, those who follow merely intellectual wisdom fall into even greater darkness of confusion.

But to the present commentator, this does not seem the true meaning; but rather that which is suggested in the verse of the Bhagavad Gita: "He who has attained self-mastery wakes where is night for all beings, and where all beings wake is night for the silent seer."

For, while it is true that those who follow after desire, completely deluded by the glamour of Maya, dwell in darkness and, in death, enter the path, not of liberation, but of bondage to Karma and recurring birth; no less true is it that the disciple, whose feet are set upon the path of wisdom and liberation, straightway enters a world which, to the deluded, is far deeper darkness; and it is just because the small old path, stretching far away, is so deeply encompassed with darkness, that the deluded shrink away from it in dread and horror, and therefore fail to see that it is the path of Light.

There is one thing, they have said, through wisdom; there is another thing, they have said, through unwisdom. Thus have we heard from the wise, who have taught us the spiritual teaching.

He who knows both, wisdom and unwisdom, he, verily, through unwisdom fording through death, through wisdom reaches the Immortal.

These two verses, which bear out the view already taken of the preceding verse, need little or no comment. Because of unwisdom, because of the delusion of Maya, because of self-centredness and bondage to personality, the majority of mankind pass through death, as men pass through the ford of a river; for such is the meaning of the word used. If they followed after wisdom, after aspiration, sacrifice, they would, even in this present life, attain to the world of immortality. Losing their lives, their personal, self-centred lives, for the sake of the Divine, they would keep them unto life everlasting. It is the teaching, old as the world, which is the very heart and essence of the great Mysteries; the secret of initiation, since the process of Initiation is that very losing, that sacrifice of the personal life, whereby the life immortal is gained and entered upon. And the practical thing would seem to be, not so much to accept this principle in a large, general way, as to carry it into effect in a multitude of little things; the little things which, like grains of sand, build mountains; like drops of water, make up the oceans.

They go forth into blind darkness, who worship that which is not the Life; but into darkness deeper than that, as it were, they who find delight in the Life.

There is one thing, they have said, through the Life; there is another thing, they have said, through that which is not the Life.

Thus have we heard from the wise, who taught us the spiritual teachings.

He who knows both, the Life and destruction, through destruction fording through death, through the Life reaches the Immortal.

There is a slight shading in the form, but not, it seems, in the meaning, of the word here translated the Life. It is a difficult word to render, meaning origin, power, production, birth, existence. Here, it seems to cover two meanings: the second birth, the spiritual birth from above, and that divine Life, the Logos, through which, and through obedience to which, the spiritual rebirth comes about.

And there seems to be a double meaning also in the word here rendered destruction. Through their following of the personality, which is the principle of destruction, since it is by its nature doomed to death, the multitude must enter the river of death, bondage to Karma and recurring birth. But there is the other and deeper meaning—for it must not be forgotten that we are dealing with a book of the Mysteries: Through the destruction, the dissolving of the personality, we cross death as those who ford a river; then, through the power of the Life, the Logos, bringing about the second birth, we reach the Immortal, in that "occult" world which, for the many, is hidden in darkness even deeper, more impenetrable, than the darkness of death.

By a veil as of gold, the face of the Real is hidden. O thou Shepherd of the flock, Lord of the sun, lift up that veil, for the vision of the law of the Real!

This is the veil of Maya, the world illusion, the world glamour. What in essence is that veil?

Let us begin with simple illustrations. We have used the word "glamour," which is the old English name of the power used by a sorcerer or witch, whether for self-concealment or to deceive in other ways; the power thus defined by the dictionary: "A magical deception of the eyes, making things appear different from what they are."

This is the power commonly known in our day as hypnotism, whereby the subject of hypnotic influence, for example, sees an onion as an apple, or takes vinegar for wine. All exercises of hypnotic power are dependent on glamour, and are, therefore, forms of sorcery and witchcraft. Our self-styled scientific age has simply changed the name, while using the same power.

This leads one naturally to self-hypnotism, which our age recognizes as a reality, though it is far indeed from realizing its scope. Self-hypnotism through the influence of desire is, indeed, fairly well understood, at least when it is operative in others; but the far more subtle self-hypnotism through the lower mind has a reach which is still almost unsuspected.

In these interpretations, we have spoken of Bergson, and of his penetrating analysis of the lower mind, as the instrument which the Life has called into being and developed, in order to deal with the material world; and the most valuable part of Bergson's work is the detailed description of the way in which the mind-machine distorts reality, in order thus to deal with it practically. Over against the mind-machine Bergson sets intuition, the power which, being a part of the Life itself, directly lays hold of the Life, and apprehends the Life as it is.

But, as we have suggested before, Bergson seems not to get at the heart of the matter, because he is inclined to consider rather the mental operation of the lower nature, without going deeply into its moral operation.

The mind-machine is, it is true, moulded and adapted to dealing with material facts, with the whole order of the material world. But Bergson passes lightly over the force, the impulse which has forced the Life in this direction, and has kept it thus bent upon the material world: the force of desire, the force called by the Buddhists "thirst," or "lust," in the general sense, as in the phrase "the lust of the eyes."

Speaking generally, then, the impelling force is the desire of the personal self, the personality, for all those things which gratify its thirst. And all these desires ultimately rest upon the lower self's desire of life, the desire to be keenly and vividly conscious of its own separate existence; a brute instinct, unreasoning, headstrong, for its own perpetuation.

And this strong brute instinct continues, having, in a sense, an existence of its own, even after considerable development of the better and more humane, because more spiritual, nature has been attained. Besides the man's truer and deeper consciousness, with its aspiration and compassion, there lingers this submerged life, desperately fighting for its own perpetuation; alert, tricky, fruitful in expedients, endlessly resourceful, and quite determined to thwart any change or development which threatens its own lease of life. This is the passional element in the lower nature, which Bergson might have analyzed and set forth to view, had he been less exclusively interested in the mental and theoretical view of life, and more interested in the practical and spiritual.

The lower personal life, the egotism, that which is often called the "personality," though this word later comes to have a better and higher meaning, has a powerful life and obstinate purposes of its own; it is, in a sense, an invader, a traitor in the camp, or, quite literally, an obsessing force, an evil spirit, to use the term of an older and simpler day.

But it is a part of the resourceful and subtle strategy of this obsessing egotism, that it largely keeps itself in hiding; lurking, as it were, below the margin of ordinary consciousness, and, from this hiding place, warping both understanding and will, for its own purposes—for the perpetuation of that low order of life and consciousness in which it can luxuriate and grow fat.

Two things, which are in reality but two aspects of the same thing, namely, spiritual vision and sacrifice, directly cut at the root of the egotism's life, threatening to draw the Life upward beyond the low level on which the egotism flourishes. Therefore the egotism is ceaselessly at war with these two things. It is the deadly enemy of spiritual vision, and of the aspiration which foreshadows spiritual vision; and therefore it ceaselessly seeks to drug and benumb the mental powers, in order to blind them to spiritual reality.

All doctrines of materialism, without any exception whatever, are due to the wakeful activity of this skilful stage-manager, who sets the scenery while himself keeping out of sight.

These doctrines of the negation of spiritual things have their ultimate root, not in some mental shortcoming or even perversity, but rather in a certain moral obliquity, in the prompting of the hidden demon who lurks in the darkness, until he is finally dragged forth into the light. Then begins a life and death struggle, which is the real drama of the soul, the theme of all mystical and religious books.

It is just because they are fighting an enemy now fully seen, that the saints recognize themselves to be "the chief of sinners." They have, through aspiration and sacrifice, stripped off the veil of this evil power; they see it in its hideousness, as it really is. And seeing, they know that they must fight to the death, overcoming, lest they be overcome. And they also know that no power or resource within the limits of their own personalities can give them the victory; nothing but the divine power of the Spirit itself, the Saviour, the Redeemer.

The saints speak with horror and loathing of this demoniac power, so long hidden but at last revealed, because they clearly see that its purpose is the death of every element of spiritual life. It seeks, quite literally, to "kill the soul," in the words of this Upanishad. And they likewise know how powerful it is, how subtle; its subtlety shown most of all in the way in which it remains concealed. Though obsessing the greater part of human life, it remains largely unsuspected, frankly disbelieved in by most people, and itself prompting that disbelief. It is well said that the devil's greatest triumph is to persuade people that there is no devil. Be it noted, by the way, that he generally persuades the same people that there is no God either, in the practical sense of a King requiring sacrifice and obedience.

The personality, in the sense we have given it, is "the veil of Maya"; that which conceals Truth, as with the lure of gold.

Who, then, is he who is to raise the veil? The name given in this Drama of the Mysteries is that of a Vedic deity, who is both a Shepherd of flocks and a Sun divinity, a Lord and Giver of Light.

The Good Shepherd, the Lord and Giver of Light—the symbolism is universal and old as life itself. That Lord and Shepherd is the Master who initiates the disciple, leading the disciple, by painful ways of sacrifice and purification, out of darkness into light, from beneath the yoke of evil into the liberty of the sons of God.

This intensely practical task is the essence and subject matter of all religion. When it is undertaken with full understanding and consciousness, it leads to full discipleship, and, in due time, to the Great Initiation, which is the subject of this Upanishad.

Therefore the Good Shepherd, the Lord and Giver of Light, is invoked, to lift the glistering veil, to give the vision of the Eternal.

Shepherd and Lord of Light, thou Only Seer, Lord of Death, Light-Giver, Son of the Lord of Life, send forth thy rays and bring them together!

That radiance of thine, thy form most beautiful I behold; the Spiritual Man in the real world. That am I!

This marks the consummation of the Great Initiation, the full vision of Divinity, wherein the consciousness of the disciple becomes one with the consciousness of the Master, and of that Master's Master and the whole ascending chain of Spiritual Life, up to and including the supreme Nirvana.

Then follows the transformation spoken of in that most mystical tract, *The Elixir of Life*, which is thus indicated in this Upanishad:

My Spirit enters the Spirit, the Immortal. And this body has its end in ashes.

There remain only the closing words, addressed to the new-born spiritual man:

O Sacrifice, remember! Remember what has been done! O Sacrifice, remember! Remember what has been done!

O Divine Fire, lead us by the good path to Victory! O Bright One, thou who knowest all wisdoms!

Give us victory over our consuming sin! To Thee we offer the highest word of praise!

Ishopanishad

Translated by Raja Ram Mohun Roy

1st. ALL the material extension in this world, whatsoever it may be, should be considered as clothed with the existence of the Supreme regulating spirit: by thus abstracting thy mind *from worldly thoughts*, preserve thyself *from self-sufficiency*, and entertain not a covetous regard for property belonging to any individual.

2nd. Let man desire to live a whole century, practising, in this world, during that time, religious rites; because for Such A SELFISH MIND AS THINE, besides the observance of these rites, there is no other mode the practice of which would not subject thee to evils.

3rd. THOSE THAT NEGLECT THE CONTEMPLATION OF THE SUPREME SPIRIT, *either by devoting themselves solely to the performance of the ceremonies of religion, or by living destitute of religious ideas, shall, after death,* ASSUME THE STATE OF DEMONS, *such as that of the celestial gods, and of other created beings,* WHICH ARE SURROUNDED WITH THE DARKNESS OF IGNORANCE.

4th. The Supreme Spirit is one and unchangeable: he proceeds more rapidly than the comprehending power of the mind: Him no external sense can apprehend, for a knowledge of him outruns even the internal sense: He, though free from motion, seems to advance, leaving behind human intellect, which strives to attain a knowledge respecting him: He being the eternal ruler, the atmosphere regulates under him the whole system of the world.

5th. He, the Supreme Being, seems to move every where, although he in reality has no motion; he seems to be distant *from those who have no wish to attain a knowledge respecting him*, and he seems to be near *to those who feel a wish to know him*: but, in fact, He pervades the internal and external parts of this whole universe.

6th. He, who perceives the whole universe in the Supreme Being (*that is, he who perceives that the material existence is merely dependent upon the existence of the Supreme Spirit*); and who also perceives the Supreme Being in the whole universe (*that is, he who perceives that the Supreme Spirit extends over all material extension*); does not feel contempt *towards any creature whatsoever.*

7th. When a person possessed of true knowledge conceives that God extends over the whole universe (*that is, that God furnishes every particle of the universe with the light of his existence*), how can he, as an observer of the real unity of the pervading Supreme existence, be affected with infatuation or grievance?

8th. He overspreads all creatures: is merely spirit, without the form either of any minute body, or of an extended one, which is liable to impression or organization: He is pure, perfect, omniscient, the ruler of the intellect, omnipresent, and the self-existent: He has from eternity been assigning to all creatures their respective purposes.

9th. Those observers of religious rites that perform only the worship of the sacred fire, and oblations to sages, to ancestors, to men, and the other creatures, without regarding the worship of celestial gods, shall enter into the dark regions: and those practisers of religious ceremonies who habitually worship the celestial gods only, disregarding the worship of the sacred fire, and oblations to sages, to ancestors, to men, and to other creatures, shall enter into a region still darker than the former.

10th. It is said that adoration of the celestial gods produces one consequence; and that the performance of the worship of sacred fire, and oblations to sages, to ancestors, to men, and to other creatures, produce another: thus have we heard from learned men who have distinctly explained the subject to us.

11th. Of those observers of ceremonies whosoever, knowing that adoration of celestial gods, as well as the worship of the sacred fire, and oblation to sages, to ancestors, to men, and to other creatures, should be observed alike by the same individual, performs them both, will, by means of the latter, surmount the obstacles presented by natural temptations, and will attain the state of the celestial gods through the practice of the former.

12th. Those observers of religious rites who worship Prakriti alone, shall enter into the dark region: and those practisers of religious ceremonies that are devoted to worship solely the prior operating sensitive particle, allegorically called Bruhma, shall enter into a region much more dark than the former.

13th. It is said that one consequence may be attained by the worship of Bruhma, and another by the adoration of Prakriti. Thus have we heard from learned men who have distinctly explained the subject to us.

14th. Of those observers of ceremonies, whatever person, knowing that the adoration of Prakriti and that of Bruhma should be together observed by the same individual, performs them both, will by means of the latter overcome indigence, and will attain the state of Prakriti, through the practice of the former.

15th. "Thou hast, O sun," (*says to the sun a person agitated on the approach of death, who during his life attended to the performance of religions rites, neglecting the attainment of a knowledge of God,*) "thou hast, O sun, concealed by thy illuminating body the way to the true Being, who rules in thee. Take off that veil for the guidance of me thy true devotee."

16th. "O thou" (continues he), "who nourishest the *world*, movest singly, and who dost regulate the whole mundane system—O sun, of Cushyup; disperse thy rays for my passage, and withdraw thy violent light, so that I may by thy grace behold thy most prosperous aspect." "*Why should I*" (*says he, again retracting himself on reflecting upon the true divine nature*) "*why should I entreat the sun, as* I AM WHAT HE IS," that is, "*the Being who rules in the sun rules also in me.*"

17th. "Let my breath," *resumes he*, "be absorbed *after death* into the wide atmosphere; and let this my body be burnt to ashes. O my intellect, think *now on what may be beneficial to me*. O fire, remember what religious rites I have hitherto performed."

18th. "O illuminating fire," *continues he*, "observing all our religious practices, carry us by the right path to the enjoyment of the consequence of our deeds, and put an end to our sins; we being now unable to perform thy various rites, offer to thee our last salutation."

www.ingramcontent.com/pod-product-compliance
Lightning Source LLC
LaVergne TN
LVHW041500070426
835507LV00009B/726